DOG DAYS

RHYMES AROUND THE YEAR

by Jack Prelutsky • illustrated by Dyanna Wolcott

ALFRED A. KNOPF • NEW YORK

JANUARY

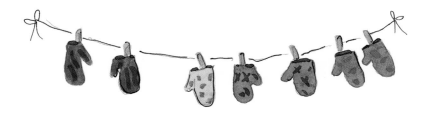

The moon is up, I rise from bed,
To glide about upon my sled.
I am a dog who finds delight
In January snow at night.

FEBRUARY

When the February rains
Beat against the windowpanes,
There is nothing I desire
But a chair and toasty fire.

MARCH

On days in March, I'm often found
Running, running all around.
It is so windy, someone's kite
Completely disappears from sight.

APRIL

April's here, I sing bow wow,
The trees are thick with blossoms now.
So as along the roads I ride,
I'm sure to have my head outside.

MAY

How sweet to be a dog in May,
And garden every single day.
I dig up dirt, I dig up stones,
And plant a row of lovely bones.

JUNE

In June I love to run and bark
With my companions in the park.
We run through picnics people made,
And overturn their lemonade.

JULY

It's very noisy in July,

When fireworks light the evening sky.

Though I'm a patriot and proud,

For ears like mine, it's much too loud.

AUGUST

In August, how I love to sail.
I yap with joy, I wag my tail,
And watch as someone else's pet
Jumps overboard and gets all wet.

SEPTEMBER

September's back, and so is school,
It's drizzling out, the morning's cool.
I do believe I'll make a fuss
When everyone gets on the bus.

OCTOBER

It's Halloween, and in the street
I'm in disguise for trick or treat.
I'm wearing what I want to wear,
And scaring who I want to scare.

NOVEMBER

It's late November, sing hooray,
For now it is Thanksgiving Day.
I do not think that I can wait
To taste that turkey on the plate.

DECEMBER

Upon a cold December day,
When at last I'm done with play,
I close my eyes and cuddle up,
And dream of when I was a pup!

In memory of Molly, Alice and Puddin, three good dogs.

—J. P.

For Willy and Sam, with a special "woof!" for Sunny.

—D. W.

THIS IS A BORZOI BOOK PUBLISHED BY ALFRED A. KNOPF, INC.

Text copyright © 1999 by Jack Prelutsky.

Illustrations copyright © 1999 by Dyanna Wolcott.

www.randomhouse.com/kids

Library of Congress Cataloging-in-Publication Data

Prelutsky, Jack.

Dog days : rhymes around the year / by Jack Prelutsky ; illustrated by Dyanna Wolcott.

p. cm.

Summary: A spirited dog describes what he enjoys doing each month of the year.

1. Dogs—Juvenile poetry. 2. Months—Juvenile poetry. 3. Children's poetry, American. [1. Dogs—Poetry.
2. Months—Poetry. 3. American Poetry.] I. Wolcott, Dyanna, ill. II. Title.

PS3566.R36D64

1999

811'.54—dc21

98-32373

ISBN 0-375-80104-9 (trade)

ISBN 0-375-90104-3 (lib. bdg.)

Printed in the United States of America

10 9 8 7 6 5 4 3 2 1